A Gift For:

_____

From:

_____

Maxine

And Another

And Another Thing
Maxine on Life, Love and Losers
Copyright 2007 Hallmark Licensing, Inc.

Published by Gift Books from Hallmark,
a division of Hallmark Cards, Inc.,
Kansas City, MO 64141
Visit us on the Web at www.Hallmark.com

Illustrations by John Wagner
Editor: Bill Moses
Art Director: Kevin Swanson
Editorial Director: Jeff Morgan
Designer: Mary Eakin
Contributing Designer: Dawn M. Weaver
Production Art: Dan C. Horton
Written by the Shoebox Humor Writing Studio

ISBN: 978-1-59530-165-9
BOK2078
Printed in China

Thing!

Maxine on Life, Love and Losers

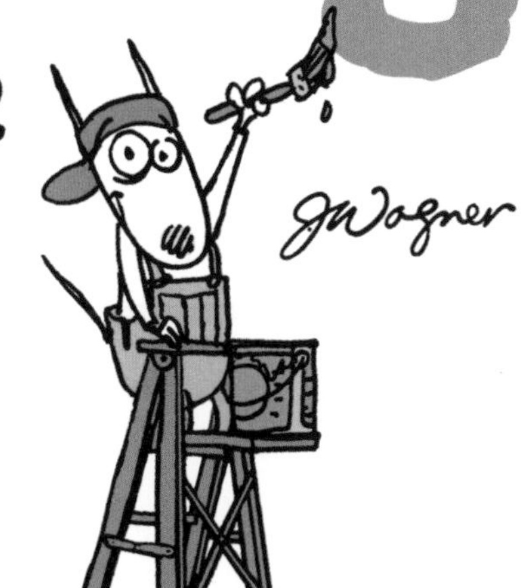

Dear Maxine Fan,

Let me tell you a secret. Just between you and me, Maxine can sometimes be, um ... a little hard to deal with. You're shocked, I know. Furthermore, if by some chance she isn't being "a little hard to deal with," it's only because she's being a SERIOUS PAIN IN THE BUTT!

There, I said it and I'm glad. And since I'm speaking my mind, you should also know that Maxine can be a real DIVA! (Boy, this feels good!) I mean, if I even hint that she isn't the one running the show around here ... well, let's just say I get an earful.

Sometimes it's good to remind myself just who draws who. I first drew Maxine for a Hallmark Shoebox™ greeting card. From that moment ... through sheer (let's call it) "force of character" ... she took on a life of her own. In fact, she pretty much took on a life of my own, too, dragging "Arty Boy" (that's me) to interviews, TV shows, conventions, book signings, charity events. You name it, we've done it—she even had her own syndicated newspaper feature. Hmm ... maybe she really is in charge.

When Maxine first arrived on my drawing board, I was surprised that she looked like my grandmother, but it seemed fitting because my grandmother was partly responsible for my career as a cartoonist. She was the one who encouraged my early doodles and paid for my first art lessons. Of course, Maxine would say, pointedly, that she can take responsibility for her own lean, mean, griping self without any help from anyone.

I had a hunch even then that people would identify with this agin' & ragin' senior who isn't afraid to yell it like it is on every subject under the ... I suppose "moon" would be appropriate. When Maxine found out that we wanted to do a book on life, love and losers, she had plenty to say. You'll see what I mean.

Uh-oh, here she comes. Gotta go ...

Your henpecked artist,

JWagner

John "Arty Boy" Wagner

Life

When I pause to look back on my life, I sometimes get *insights*, sometimes *wisdom*, and sometimes a sense of *perspective*. Of course, the only thing I'm sure to get is a crick in my neck...and that really *sets me off!* Lucky for you, I already got that part out of the way...

I've got the ergonomic office chair, but the job's still a pain in the butt.
Maxine

I tried getting away from it all. Most of it followed me.

Never put off till tomorrow what you can just ignore indefinitely.

The journey of ten feet begins with a single "Where's the ♥%*#&! remote?"

Love

Standards, expectations, goals, dreams ...
at this point in my love life, my boobs aren't the only things
that are lower than they used to be. If you're in the same
boat (the same *sinking* boat) read on ...

Snowmen and real men have a lot in common. For one thing, it would take some kind of magic hat to get either of them off their asses.

Men—can't live with them,
can't watch somebody pick their teeth
with a matchbook without them.

After a romantic encounter, I always do the same thing ... belch and put the lid back on the chocolates.

I wouldn't want to underestimate men. Fortunately, that's not possible.

If men are from Mars,
we need to find the
bozo who supplied them
with spaceships.

Losers

I'll admit that sometimes I let the stupid little things get to me. And I don't handle the average ones or the tall ones very well either. Can you sympathize? Well, that's your problem right there. My advice is to start letting people know how you really feel ...

There's no fool like
an old fool ...
but the young ones
are coming along.

Time for a prank call. Think I'll call the phone company and tell 'em the check's in the mail.

My boss asked me to take an anger management class this year. I told him I'm angry enough with management as it is.

It's tough being a congressman.
If you don't believe me, you try patting
yourself on the back with both hands
in constituents' pockets.

Good fences make good neighbors. Electric fences make great neighbors.

The early bird may get the worm, but the night owl gets the tequila!

If you don't have anything nice to say, you can probably get a job in human resources.